Individual Reading Inventory

Scott Foresman

Editorial Offices: Glenview, Illinois • New York, New York
Sales Offices: Reading, Massachusetts • Duluth, Georgia • Glenview, Illinois
Carrollton, Texas • Menlo Park, California

Editorial Offices
Glenview, Illinois • New York, New York

Sales Offices
Reading, Massachusetts • Duluth, Georgia • Glenview, Illinois
Carrollton, Texas • Menlo Park, California

ISBN 0-673-64055-8

2 3 4 5 6 7 8 9 10-ML-06 05 04 03 02 01 00

CONTENTS

OVERVIEW

Scott Foresman Reading provides a wide array of group-administered formal tests and classroom assessments to support instruction, including Placement Tests, Selection Tests, Skills Tests, and Benchmark Tests. This booklet provides information and directions for administering and scoring the Individual Reading Inventory, which is an individual assessment of reading and language concepts.

The primary purpose of the Individual Reading Inventory (IRI) is to help you collect information about individual students' reading and language development. This information can be used to make instructional decisions about each student, identify specific strengths and weaknesses, and assess students' progress throughout the year.

The IRI is designed to measure reading comprehension and oral reading. Comprehension may be assessed with the use of comprehension questions or a retelling, or both. Oral reading may be assessed with the use of a Running Record.

This booklet provides a description of the IRI, directions for administering the IRI, a series of grade-level reading passages for Grades 3–6, and evaluation charts that may be copied for recording the results of assessments.

The reading passages include four passages for Grade 3 (numbered 1–4) and two passages per grade for Grades 4, 5, and 6 (numbered 1–2 in each grade). The first passage in each grade is a fiction selection, and the second passage is nonfiction. In Grade 3, passages 1 and 3 are fiction, and passages 2 and 4 are nonfiction.

For each reading passage, this booklet includes a Student Page and a Teacher Page. The reading passage appears on the Student Page. The Teacher Page provides a set of comprehension questions, criteria for evaluating a retelling, and data to help in taking a Running Record.

Using the Materials in This Book

The IRI may be used in several ways to collect information about individual students and thus support placement decisions and help plan instruction. Any and all of the passages may be used to administer comprehension questions, a retelling, or a Running Record. For most students, we recommend the following procedure:

1. Administer the Individual Reading Inventory by having the student read Passage 1 at the appropriate grade level. Have the student read silently and answer the comprehension questions orally. If the results of this assessment are not conclusive, then . . .

2. Have the student retell the story. If the results of this assessment are not conclusive, then . . .

3. Give the student Passage 2. Have the student read Passage 2 aloud. As the student reads, take a Running Record. Then have the student retell the story and answer the comprehension questions.

For students who excel in the assessment at a specific grade level, you may want to collect additional information by administering passages at higher levels. Information from above-grade-level assessments can help you plan challenging activities for instruction.

The following section provides a description of each assessment and how to administer it.

DIRECTIONS FOR ADMINISTERING THE IRI

The Individual Reading Inventory (IRI) is primarily an assessment of reading comprehension. For each reading passage in this booklet, the Teacher Page provides a set of five comprehension questions and correct answers. The student reads the passage aloud or silently and then answers the questions.

Comprehending and Responding

To administer the basic IRI, follow this procedure:

1. At the appropriate grade level, make a copy of the Student Page for Passage 1 and the Teacher Page for Passage 1.

2. Give the Student Page to the student and have the student read the passage silently.

3. When the student has finished, read each comprehension question aloud from the Teacher Page and have the student answer it. Record the results of the assessment on the Teacher Page by marking the answer to each of the five questions as correct or incorrect.

4. If the student answers only two or three of the questions correctly, you may want to have the student retell the story and record your observations on the Teacher Page.

Interpreting the Results

If the student answers one, two, or three of the questions correctly, then the student may need considerable instructional guidance or intervention. You will probably need to administer additional assessments to identify the student's instructional needs. In addition to having students retell the story, we recommend proceeding with Passage 2 at the same grade level and taking a Running Record.

If the student answers four of the five questions correctly, then the student will likely benefit from instructional guidance at the targeted grade level. You may end the assessment here, continue with the IRI by administering Passage 2, or administer other assessments to collect more information.

If the student answers all five questions correctly, then the student will likely need additional challenge in instruction. We recommend administering the IRI for the next higher level(s) to help identify more specific needs.

Retelling

A retelling is also an assessment of reading comprehension. For each reading passage in this booklet, the Teacher Page provides a set of criteria for observing and evaluating a student's retelling of the literature selection. The student reads the passage aloud or silently; then he or she retells the story in a fiction selection or recounts the most important information in a nonfiction passage.

To administer a retelling after the student has answered the comprehension questions, ask him or her to retell the selection. Use the criteria in the Retelling box on the Teacher Page to record the results. If the student has difficulty retelling the selection or omits important information, you may want to prompt the student to tell you more about specific parts of the selection.

Interpreting the Results

A retelling is most helpful for identifying what the student understands and does not understand about a particular selection. The results should usually be evaluated in relation to other assessments, especially if the student has already answered the comprehension questions for the passage. Since some students may respond better to retelling or to answering specific questions, the combination of the two approaches will provide more comprehensive information about the student's instructional needs.

HOW TO TAKE A RUNNING RECORD

A Running Record is an assessment of oral reading accuracy and oral reading fluency. A student's reading accuracy is based on the number of words read correctly. This measure is determined by an analysis of the errors a student makes — a miscue analysis. Reading fluency is based on reading rate (the number of words read per minute) and the degree to which the student reads with a "natural flow."

A Running Record may be taken using any reading selection at any time. However, the most valid and reliable assessment fulfills these requirements: (1) the text is appropriate to the student's reading level and interest; (2) the text is unfamiliar to the student. The passages in this booklet are well-suited for use with a Running Record because they fit these requirements. For additional administrations that involve a Running Record, you may choose other passages from grade-level appropriate texts.

The Running Record may be used to verify instructional decisions suggested by other assessments, such as a Placement Test. It may also be used to identify a student's particular strengths and weaknesses in reading and language development. In addition, the Running Record may be administered periodically throughout the year as a means of monitoring a student's progress.

Measuring oral reading accuracy and oral reading fluency may be accomplished in a single reading, but two different operations are required. The guidelines below explain how to determine each measurement.

How to Measure Oral Reading Accuracy

1. Choose an appropriate grade-level text of about 100 to 200 words.

2. Make two copies of the text—one for the student and one for you. If the text appears in a book, you may have the student read the text from the book.

3. Give the text to the student and have the student read the text aloud. (You may want to tape-record the student's reading for later evaluation. This approach can be especially helpful if you are timing the student's reading or conducting other assessments at the same time.)

4. On your copy of the text, mark any miscues or errors the student makes during the reading (see the explanation of reading miscues/errors below).

5. Count the total number of errors the student makes and find the percentage score for the number of errors. If you are using a passage from this book, the Teacher Page for that passage tells the number of words in the passage and provides a table for determining a percentage score.

6. If you are using a text from a different source, use this formula to get a percentage score:

$$\frac{\text{Total \# of words} - \text{\# of errors}}{\text{Total \# of words}} \times 100 = \text{percentage score}$$

Example: Suppose a student reads a text of 110 words and makes 6 errors.

$$\frac{110 - 6 = 104 \text{ words}}{110} = 0.945 \qquad 0.945 \times 100 = 94.5\% \text{ (round to 95\%)}$$

Whether you use the table provided or calculate the percentage yourself, the percentage score indicates the student's oral reading accuracy (percentage of words in the passage read correctly).

How to Identify Reading Miscues/Errors

The chart below shows the kinds of miscues or errors to look for as a student reads aloud and the notations used to mark them.

Reading Miscue	Notations
Omission The student omits words or word parts.	The detective rushed into ⟨the⟩ store.
Substitution The student substitutes words or parts of words for the words in the text.	_ran_ The detective ~~rushed~~ into the store.
Insertion The student inserts words or parts of words that are not in the text.	_nice_ Linda wanted to buy them a ∧ present.
Mispronunciation/Misreading The student pronounces or reads a word incorrectly.	_boy_ Linda wanted to buy them a present.
Hesitation The student hesitates over a word and the teacher provides the word.	_H_ Paul grabbed the <u>turnip</u> and pulled.
Self-Correction The student reads a word incorrectly but then corrects the error.	⟨SC⟩ The turnip flew out of the ground.

Notes

- If the student hesitates over a word, wait several seconds before identifying it for the student.
- If a student makes the same error more than once, count it as only one error. For example, if the student mispronounces _calendar_ three times, count it as one error.
- Self-correction is not counted as an actual error. However, writing "SC" over the word or words will help you identify words that give the student some difficulty.

How to Measure Reading Rate

Reading rate is generally defined as number of words per minute (wpm). To determine the reading rate, follow steps 1–3 as described on page 4. Note the exact time when the student begins reading and the time when he or she finishes.

To calculate the number of words per minute, use the formula below:

$$\frac{\text{Total \# of words read}}{\text{\# of seconds}} \times 60 = \text{words per minute}$$

Example: Suppose a child reads a passage of 120 words in 90 seconds.

$$\frac{120}{90} = 1.33$$

$$1.33 \times 60 = 79.8 \text{ words per minute (round to 80)}$$

The sample passage on the next page shows the errors a student made in reading a text. For each error, the teacher made a notation. The teacher also noted the amount of time it took the student to read the text.

> **Total words in passage: 140**
> **Total number of errors: 8**
> **Time of reading: 90 seconds**

Reading accuracy:

$$\frac{140 - 8}{140} = 0.943 \times 100 = 94.3, \text{ or } 94\%$$

Reading rate:

$$\frac{140}{90} = 1.56 \times 60 = 93.6, \text{ or } 94 \text{ words per minute}$$

Sample

Lisa wanted to buy her parents a present for their wedding anniversary. She decided to buy them a clock radio. The radio cost thirty dollars, but Lisa had only ten dollars.

Lisa needed twenty dollars. She couldn't ask her brother for the money because he was saving for a bike. Lisa would have to earn the money herself.

She tried to think of some ideas. She couldn't mow lawns because it was the wrong season. She couldn't baby-sit because she was too young.

Just then her dog barked. "Okay," said Lisa, "I'll take you for a walk." She looked outside and saw that it had started to snow. She hated taking her dog for a walk on cold days. Suddenly she knew how she could earn the money. Other dog owners probably didn't like going out in bad weather either.

Time: 1 Min, 30 Sec

Interpreting the Results

For oral reading accuracy, use the following criteria:

- A student who reads 98%–100% of the words correctly is reading at an independent level and may need more challenging texts.

- A student who reads 91%–97% of the words correctly is reading at an instructional level and will likely benefit from guided instruction in the regular program.

- A student who reads with an accuracy of 90% or less is reading at a frustration level and may benefit most from targeted instruction with lower-level texts or intervention.

For oral reading fluency, an appropriate reading rate is roughly equal to the student's age X 10, plus or minus 10. Thus, a student who is eight years old should be able to read 70–90 words per minute The chart below shows the expected reading rate for each age level.

Age	Reading Rate (wpm)	Age	Reading Rate (wpm)
7	60–80	11	100–120
8	70–90	12	110–130
9	80–100	13	120–140
10	90–110	14	130–150

A child who is reading below the expected reading rate may benefit most from targeted instruction and practice with lower-level texts.

For any student whose Running Record results are not clearly definitive, we recommend administering additional individual assessments, such as classroom observations and anecdotal records. For more information about other assessments, refer to the *Assessment Handbook.*

Evaluation Chart

The chart on the next page can be copied and used to help record and evaluate assessment results. Make a copy of the Individual Assessment Chart for each student. Use it to record the student's results on any or all three of the assessments.

EVALUATION CHART

Student ____

Teacher ____

Level/Passages	Date	Comprehension		Running Record Accuracy	Fluency
Grade 3					
Passage 1		/5	%	%	(wpm)
Passage 2		/5	%	%	(wpm)
Passage 3		/5	%	%	(wpm)
Passage 4		/5	%	%	(wpm)
Grade 4					
Passage 1		/5	%	%	(wpm)
Passage 2		/5	%	%	(wpm)
Grade 5					
Passage 1		/5	%	%	(wpm)
Passage 2		/5	%	%	(wpm)
Grade 6					
Passage 1		/5	%	%	(wpm)
Passage 2		/5	%	%	(wpm)

Notes/Observations

Lisa wanted to buy her parents a present for their wedding anniversary. She decided to buy them a clock radio. The radio cost thirty dollars, but Lisa had only ten dollars.

Lisa needed twenty dollars. She couldn't ask her brother for the money because he was saving for a bike. Lisa would have to earn the money herself.

She tried to think of some ideas. She couldn't mow lawns because it was the wrong season. She couldn't baby-sit because she was too young.

Just then her dog barked. "Okay," said Lisa, "I'll take you for a walk." She looked outside and saw that it had started to snow. She hated taking her dog for a walk on cold days. Suddenly she knew how she could earn the money. Other dog owners probably didn't like going out in bad weather either.

Grade 3
Passage 1

Teacher Page

Questions

1. **Why did Lisa want to give her parents a clock radio?**
   It was a present for their anniversary, or their anniversary was coming up.

2. **Why didn't Lisa ask her brother for the money she needed?**
   He was saving his money to buy a bike.

3. **How can you tell what time of year this story takes place?**
   It was snowing out, and/or it was the wrong season for mowing lawns.

4. **Lisa thought about mowing lawns. What does "mow lawns" mean?**
   "cut the grass," or something similar

5. **What do you think Lisa will do to earn the money she needs?**
   She will start a pet-walking business, or she will walk the neighbors' dogs in bad weather.

Reading Comprehension		Oral Reading Accuracy		Oral Reading Fluency	
No. Correct	Percent	# of Errors	% Score	Time	Rate (wpm)
/5	%				

Retelling

Initial retelling included:

___ characters
___ setting
___ important details
___ events in sequence
___ vocabulary/phrases from story
___ events out of sequence
___ ending

Was the initial retelling complete? ______
If not, did you prompt the student to add
  information? ______
Did the student add details
  upon prompting? ______

Oral Reading Accuracy	
Number of Words: 140	
# of Errors	Percent
1–2	99
3	98
4	97
5–6	96
7	95
8–9	94
10	93
11	92
12–13	91
14	90

A violin is a stringed musical instrument that is made of wood. To play a violin, the musician uses both hands. The fingers of one hand press the strings, and the other hand pulls a bow across the strings.

The first violins were made in the 1500s. A few families became very famous as violin makers. They made the best violins. They experimented with the way violins were made. Slowly, the violin was changed into the instrument that people enjoy today.

A violin can sound like a screeching bird the first time you try to play it! If you practice hard, though, you may learn to make music that is rich and deep, or light and happy. Many people play violins today.

Questions

1. **Why would someone want a violin?**
   to make music, or to play it

2. **How can you tell that people have been playing violins for a long time?**
   The first violins were made in the 1500s.

3. **The selection says violin makers experimented. What does "experimented" mean?**
   They tried out new things, or tested different ways of making violins.

4. **Why did some families become famous for their violins?**
   They made the best ones, or they made good violins.

5. **How can you tell that it takes a long time to learn to play the violin well?**
   The selection says you must practice hard to make beautiful music, or a violin can sound like a screeching bird the first time you try to play it.

Reading Comprehension		Oral Reading Accuracy		Oral Reading Fluency	
No. Correct	Percent	# of Errors	% Score	Time	Rate (wpm)
/5	%				

Retelling

Initial retelling included:

___ main topic
___ events or ideas in sequence
___ important details
___ events/ideas out of sequence
___ vocabulary/phrases from text
___ conclusion(s) based on text

Was the initial retelling complete? ______
If not, did you prompt the student to add
   information? ______
Did the student add details
   upon prompting? ______

Oral Reading Accuracy	
Number of Words: 122	
# of Errors	Percent
1	99
2–3	98
4	97
5	96
6	95
7	94
8–9	93
10	92
11	91
12	90

It was Sheila's first time. She would use a rope to go backwards down a steep cliff that no one could climb.

Sheila fastened her helmet. She wore thick gloves and heavy overalls so the rope wouldn't burn her skin. Standing between a tree and the edge of a cliff, she picked up some rope. One end was wrapped tightly around the tree. The other end had been thrown over the edge to the bottom of the cliff. Her teacher wrapped the rope securely around her body. Sheila faced the tree. She was ready, but she knew the hardest part would be taking that first step. For a moment she stood frozen on the edge of the cliff. Then she took a deep breath and stepped backwards.

She felt her boot touch the wall of the cliff and the rope slide through her hand. She was doing it! Within a few minutes Sheila's feet touched the ground. She did a little dance and laughed out loud.

Grade 3
Passage 3

Teacher Page

Questions

1. **What was Sheila doing for the first time?**
   She was going down a cliff with a rope.

2. **How did she probably feel when she was standing on top of the cliff?**
   scared, nervous, or frightened

3. **The story says that Sheila wore heavy overalls. What are "overalls"?**
   a kind of clothing, or pants, or a one-piece suit

4. **How do you know that Sheila went down the rope correctly?**
   Her feet touched the ground.

5. **How did Sheila probably feel about herself when she reached the ground?**
   proud, glad, or relieved

Reading Comprehension		Oral Reading Accuracy		Oral Reading Fluency	
No. Correct	Percent	# of Errors	% Score	Time	Rate (wpm)
/5	%				

Retelling

Initial retelling included:

___ characters
___ setting
___ important details
___ events in sequence
___ vocabulary/phrases from story
___ events out of sequence
___ ending

Was the initial retelling complete? ______
If not, did you prompt the student to add
   information? ______
Did the student add details
   upon prompting? ______

Oral Reading Accuracy	
Number of Words: 166	
# of Errors	Percent
1–2	99
3–4	98
5	97
6–7	96
8	95
9–10	94
11–12	93
13	92
14–15	91
16	90

Many years ago, silver plates and bowls were made by hand. Making a bowl out of silver was not an easy job.

The silversmith started with a flat sheet of silver. With a sharp pair of snips, he cut out the basic shape of the bowl. Then he marked circles on the flat cutout. These circles showed him where to hammer. Small circles were for the bottom. Larger circles were for the sides.

Next, he hammered and formed the bowl. For a worktable, he used a large block of wood with hollows carved into it. He placed his cutout over a hollow that was shaped like a bowl. Then he carefully began to hammer.

He smoothed the surface of the bowl with taps of a small hammer. When the surface was smooth, designs were added to the sides of the bowl.

The last step was to polish the bowl with a rough paste. This made the bowl as shiny as a mirror.

Grade 3
Passage 4

Teacher Page

Questions

1. **To make a bowl, what did the silversmith do first?**
   He cut out the basic shape from a sheet of silver.

2. **The selection says the silversmith used a pair of snips. What are "snips" used for?**
   cutting metal

3. **How did the silversmith form the bowl?**
   He placed the silver cutout over a hollow and hammered the silver into shape.

4. **What did he do after smoothing the surface?**
   He added designs to the sides.

5. **What was the rough paste used for?**
   to polish the bowl

Reading Comprehension		Oral Reading Accuracy		Oral Reading Fluency	
No. Correct	Percent	# of Errors	% Score	Time	Rate (wpm)
/5	%				

Retelling

Initial retelling included:

___ main topic
___ events or ideas in sequence
___ important details
___ events/ideas out of sequence
___ vocabulary/phrases from text
___ conclusion(s) based on text

Was the initial retelling complete? ______
If not, did you prompt the student to add
   information? ______
Did the student add details
   upon prompting? ______

Oral Reading Accuracy	
Number of Words: 162	
# of Errors	Percent
1–2	99
3–4	98
5	97
6–7	96
8	95
9–10	94
11–12	93
13	92
14–15	91
16	90

Pinnacle Pam was the tallest girl in town, even taller than Holbrook's Department Store, which towered eight stories high! Pam liked to exercise her long legs by taking a morning jog around the world—twice.

One day after running around the planet, Pinnacle Pam arrived home quite hot and thirsty. "I'll take a nice long drink from the lake," she said. In one stride she had left the center of town and reached the lakeside. Soon Pam had drunk the whole lake dry!

The townspeople were shocked when they discovered there was no water to water the gardens with, no water to bathe in, and no water to drink.

Then Pam's little brother Pete, who knew that Pam loved jokes, began to whisper in her ear. Pam giggled. Then she laughed. Finally she was laughing so hard that tears streamed down her cheeks. Tears gushed from her eyes in such a flood that the lake was quickly filled once again.

Grade 4
Passage 1

Teacher Page

Questions

1. **What did Pinnacle Pam like to do for exercise?**
   She liked to jog around the world (twice).

2. **How was Pinnacle Pam different from everyone else in town?**
   She was taller than everyone.

3. **Why were the townspeole shocked?**
   The lake was dry, or there was no water in the lake.

4. **In the story, Pam took one stride. What is a "stride"?**
   a long step

5. **How did the lake get filled up with water?**
   Pinnacle Pam cried a flood of tears.

°Reading Comprehension		Oral Reading Accuracy		Oral Reading Fluency	
No. Correct	Percent	# of Errors	% Score	Time	Rate (wpm)
/5	%				

Retelling

Initial retelling included:

____ characters
____ setting
____ important details
____ events in sequence
____ vocabulary/phrases from story
____ events out of sequence
____ ending

Was the initial retelling complete? ______
If not, did you prompt the student to add
   information? ______
Did the student add details
   upon prompting? ______

Oral Reading Accuracy	
Number of Words: 160	
# of Errors	Percent
1–2	99
3	98
4–5	97
6	96
7–8	95
9	94
10–11	93
12	92
13–14	91
15	90

One of the largest animals that ever lived was the Brontosaurus. It weighed about forty tons, and it stretched as long as seventy feet from the top of its head to the end of its tail.

The name Brontosaurus means "thunder lizard." The name comes from the notion that the ground "thundered" when this enormous reptile walked on it.

For its large size, though, Brontosaurus was a gentle dinosaur. It never attacked other dinosaurs because it had no way to fight. It spent all its time standing in the shallow part of rivers and lakes, lazily chewing plants. Many of the other dinosaurs that lived around Brontosaurus had long sharp teeth and were always hungry for meat. When one of these enemies approached Brontosaurus, the huge animal just lumbered farther out into the water. The "thunder lizard" was safe if the water was deep enough to prevent the enemy from following.

Grade 4
Passage 2

Teacher Page

Questions

1. **Why was Brontosaurus named "thunder lizard"?**
   The ground thundered when it walked.

2. **Why didn't Brontosaurus attack other dinosaurs?**
   It had no way to fight, or it did not eat meat.

3. **The selection says the animal lumbered away. What does "lumbered" mean?**
   walked heavily, or moved clumsily

4. **How did Brontosaurus escape from danger?**
   It walked out into deep water where its enemies could not follow.

5. **What was one way Brontosaurus was different from its enemies?**
   It was gentle; it ate plants instead of meat; it had no way to fight.

Reading Comprehension		Oral Reading Accuracy		Oral Reading Fluency	
No. Correct	Percent	# of Errors	% Score	Time	Rate (wpm)
/5	%				

Retelling

Initial retelling included:

____ main topic
____ events or ideas in sequence
____ important details
____ events/ideas out of sequence
____ vocabulary/phrases from text
____ conclusion(s) based on text

Was the initial retelling complete? ______
If not, did you prompt the student to add
   information? ______
Did the student add details
   upon prompting? ______

Oral Reading Accuracy	
Number of Words: 151	
# of Errors	Percent
1–2	99
3	98
4–5	97
6	96
7–8	95
9	94
10–11	93
12	92
13–14	91
15	90

Duke always liked Grandmother Yang's gifts. She knew he loved music, and her presents showed it. But this time, she gave Duke a plant with green flowers and pink leaves. Plants meant nothing to Duke, but Grandmother loved them. When Grandmother left, she pointed to the plant and said, "It carries a tune beautifully."

Puzzled, Duke took the plant to his window and watered it with ice water he'd left on his desk.

"That's cold," a voice cried, "and this light is too bright."

Feeling silly, Duke replied, "Granny never said her plants could talk."

"She knows how to care for us, so we don't have to," replied the plant.

"This is crazy," Duke sputtered. "I'm talking to a dumb old plant!" At this insult, the plant began to droop. "Oh, I'm sorry," Duke apologized. "What do you need?"

The plant perked right up. "I need a warm, bright spot, but not in the sun," it said. "Also, I need watering with cool water, and a bigger pot."

"Okay," Duke laughed, "but what do I get?"

The plant opened its flowers and Duke heard lovely music.

"Grandmother always does give great presents," Duke said with a smile.

Grade 5
Passage 1   Teacher Page

Questions

1. **Why did Grandmother Yang think Duke would like the plant?**
   It played or sang beautifully; she knew he loved music.

2. **Why was Duke puzzled when he got the plant?**
   He expected something musical; he did not know it produced music; or Granny said it carried a tune beautifully.

3. **How did Duke first discover that the plant was unusual?**
   When he put cold water on it, the plant talked.

4. **The story says that the plant "perked right up." What does that mean?**
   looked healthy again, or became lively again

5. **What did the plant offer to Duke in return for better care?**
   beautiful music (and flowers)

Reading Comprehension		Oral Reading Accuracy		Oral Reading Fluency	
No. Correct	Percent	# of Errors	% Score	Time	Rate (wpm)
/5	%				

Retelling

Initial retelling included:

___ characters
___ setting
___ important details
___ events in sequence
___ vocabulary/phrases from story
___ events out of sequence
___ ending

Was the initial retelling complete? ______
If not, did you prompt the student to add
   information? ______
Did the student add details
   upon prompting? ______

Oral Reading Accuracy	
Number of Words: 197	
# of Errors	Percent
1–2	99
3–4	98
5–6	97
7–8	96
9–10	95
11–12	94
13–14	93
15–16	92
17–18	91
19–20	90

Meteors are glowing bits of matter that streak across the sky. They are often called falling stars or shooting stars because they look like stars falling to the Earth. Meteors become visible when they enter the Earth's atmosphere. In this layer of air, the meteors travel along at speeds of up to 49 miles per second. Friction with the air makes the meteor so hot it glows, leaving a trail of hot, glowing gases behind it. Most meteors rarely glow for more than a few seconds.

Scientists estimate that as many 200 million meteors are visible in the Earth's atmosphere each day. We first see most of these meteors when they are about 65 miles above the Earth. They burn out at altitudes of 30 to 50 miles. Most meteors are no larger than a grain of sand.

Questions

1. **What is another name for a meteor?**
   falling star or shooting star

2. **What causes a meteor to glow?**
   Friction with the air makes the meteor hot, causing it to glow.

3. **The selection says that meteors become visible. What does "visible" mean?**
   able to be seen

4. **Where do meteors come from?**
   beyond the Earth's atmosphere, or outer space

5. **Why don't most meteors reach the surface of the Earth?**
   They are so small that they burn out before they reach the Earth.

Reading Comprehension		Oral Reading Accuracy		Oral Reading Fluency	
No. Correct	Percent	# of Errors	% Score	Time	Rate (wpm)
/5	%				

Retelling

Initial retelling included:

___ main topic
___ events or ideas in sequence
___ important details
___ events/ideas out of sequence
___ vocabulary/phrases from text
___ conclusion(s) based on text

Was the initial retelling complete? ______
If not, did you prompt the student to add
   information? ______
Did the student add details
   upon prompting? ______

Oral Reading Accuracy	
Number of Words: 137	
# of Errors	Percent
1–2	99
3	98
4	97
5–6	96
7	95
8	94
9–10	93
11	92
12–13	91
14	90

A poor, old fiddler was trudging home late one night through a forest when he met a little man in a red cap. "Come and play at a wedding dance," the man requested.

"My old fingers are stiff and I do not play well," said the fiddler. "My fiddle, too, is ruined."

"Play with a generous heart and you'll play well enough!" said the little man. He led the fiddler to a lighted cave deep in the forest and then guided him down through a tunnel to a splendid hall. Soon hundreds of tiny people were crowding around the fiddler crying, "Play us a waltz."

Remembering that the man had only asked that he play with a generous heart, the fiddler began to play. To his amazement, his stiff hands felt strong. His broken fiddle was now a splendid violin! All night the rich tones of his music filled the hall.

When morning broke, the little people proclaimed, "With such a generous heart, you will always play as well and as happily as you have played tonight." And so it was, for the fiddler with the fine violin from then on played in great mansions and palaces across the land.

Grade 6
Passage 1   Teacher Page

Questions

1. **Where does the fiddler meet the little man?**
   in a forest

2. **Why did the little man want the fiddler to come to the cave?**
   He wanted the fiddler to play at a wedding dance.

3. **The little people said, "Play us a waltz." What is a waltz?**
   a kind of song or music, or a kind of dance

4. **Why was the old fiddler suddenly able to play beautiful music?**
   He played with a generous heart.

5. **What was one way the old fiddler was different after his night in the cave?**
   He could play beautiful music, his hands were strong again, and his old fiddle was a fine violin.

Reading Comprehension		Oral Reading Accuracy		Oral Reading Fluency	
No. Correct	Percent	# of Errors	% Score	Time	Rate (wpm)
/5	%				

Retelling

Initial retelling included:

___ characters
___ setting
___ important details
___ events in sequence
___ vocabulary/phrases from story
___ events out of sequence
___ ending

Was the initial retelling complete? ______
If not, did you prompt the student to add information? ______
Did the student add details upon prompting? ______

Oral Reading Accuracy	
Number of Words: 200	
# of Errors	Percent
1–2	99
3–4	98
5–6	97
7–8	96
9–10	95
11–12	94
13–14	93
15–16	92
17–18	91
19–20	90

Have you ever wondered what people did for entertainment before television was invented? The answer is radio.

Today's radio programs mostly play music or report the news or sports events. Some stations broadcast talk shows. Today's programs hardly compare to what radio was like before television.

"The Golden Age of Radio" describes the years when thousands of people gathered around their living-room radios. They would listen to comedy, adventure, western, or police shows in much the same way people today watch television.

The creators of radio shows used their imaginations to set the right atmosphere for each story. Sound-effects specialists used a variety of techniques to set scenes. They made the sound of thunder by slapping two boards together. Shaking dried beans in a metal pan sounded like rain. Coconut shells were used to create the sound of horses' hooves.

Listeners used their own imaginations to form pictures of the action in their minds. Each person would create a different picture from the descriptions and conversations on the show.

The radio shows that are best remembered are those that made people get involved. Unlike the wonderful old radio shows, television doesn't require people to use their imaginations.

Grade 6
Passage 2

Teacher Page

Questions

1. **What did people do for entertainment during "The Golden Age of Radio"?**
   They listened to radio shows.

2. **What did creators of radio shows use sound effects for?**
   to set the atmosphere for each story, or to make stories sound real

3. **Sound-effects specialists used a variety of techniques. What is another word for "techniques"?**
   methods or procedures

4. **What kind of radio shows are best remembered today?**
   shows that got people involved

5. **According to the writer of this selection, how were radio shows better than TV shows?**
   Radio shows required the use of imagination, or they got people involved.

Reading Comprehension		Oral Reading Accuracy		Oral Reading Fluency	
No. Correct	Percent	# of Errors	% Score	Time	Rate (wpm)
/5	%				

Retelling

Initial retelling included:

___ main topic
___ events or ideas in sequence
___ important details
___ events/ideas out of sequence
___ vocabulary/phrases from text
___ conclusion(s) based on text

Was the initial retelling complete? ______
If not, did you prompt the student to add
   information? ______
Did the student add details
   upon prompting? ______

Oral Reading Accuracy	
Number of Words: 197	
# of Errors	Percent
1–2	99
3–4	98
5–6	97
7–8	96
9–10	95
11–12	94
13–14	93
15–16	92
17–18	91
19–20	90